OPPOSITES

ISBN 0-590-06218-2

Copyright © 1986 by Rosalinda Kightley.
All rights reserved. Published by Scholastic Inc., 555 Broadway, New York, NY 10012, by arrangement with Little, Brown and Company (Inc.).
TRUMPET and the TRUMPET logo are registered trademarks of Scholastic Inc.

12 11 10 9 8 7 6 5   6 7 8 9/0

Printed in the U.S.A.

OPPOSITES

ROSALINDA KIGHTLEY

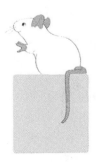

A TRUMPET CLUB SPECIAL EDITION

up

down

happy

sad

in

out

hot

cold

under

over

open

shut

dry

wet

hard

soft

big

little

full

empty

day

night

Can you find the opposites?

full

sad

hot

little

under

out

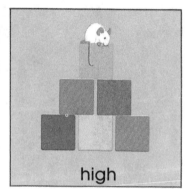

high

shut

hard

night

up

wet

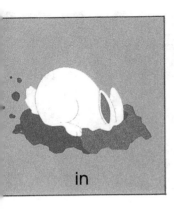

in

low

dry

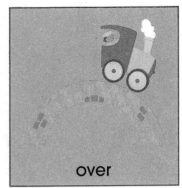

over

open

cold

happy

down

big

empty

day

soft

up   down

happy   sad

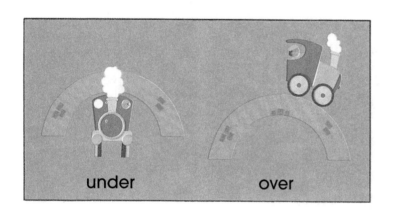

under   over

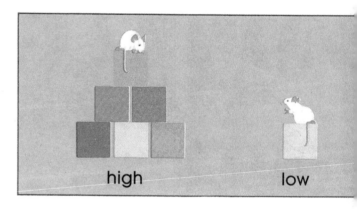

high   low

hard   soft

big   little

in   out

hot   cold

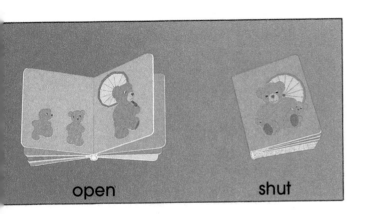

open   shut

dry   wet

full   empty

day   night